BEYOND THE CLASSROOM

MATH IN YOUR LIFE

by Charis Mather

BEARPORT PUBLISHING

Fusion Books, an imprint of Bearport Publishing by FlutterBee

Credits
All images are courtesy of Shutterstock.com, unless otherwise specified. With thanks to Getty Images, Thinkstock Photo, and iStockphoto. Cover, © Line By Line Vectors, Dmitr1ch, Bohdan Malitskiy, Voin_Sveta, Dilen, Inactive design, M_Videous, Stokkete, Ganzyk, Chaosamran_Studio, Red Vector, xphar, Bankrx. Throughout, © Line By Line Vectors, Dmitr1ch, SkyPics Studio; 4–5, © Hananeko_Studio, SkyPics Studio, Yuricazac; 6–7, © jittawit21, ShineTerra, Ground Picture, Eleonora_os; 8–9, © LightField Studios, ViJul, KutuzovaDesign, Witanto Gallery; 10–11, © Roman Samborskyi, AstroStar, Fineart1, Monkey Business Images, Ground Picture, Iris vector; 12–13, © ESB Professional, Arvind Balaraman; 14–15, © wavebreakmedia, Brian A Jackson, Aleksandr_Lysenko; 16–17, © Monkey Business Images, AlexLab; 18–19, © VH-studio, Cineberg, Kucher Serhii, testing, Wise ant, Babka; 20–21, © AnnaStills, Blend Images - JGI/Jamie Grill; 22–23, © Akkalak Aiempradit, Jayakri, Alena Nv.

Bearport Publishing Company Product Development Team
Kayla Eggert, Theresa Emminizer, Kim Jones, Allison Juda, Cole Nelson, Naomi Reich, Steve Scheluchin, Tiana Tran

Library of Congress Cataloging-in-Publication Data is available at www.loc.gov or upon request from the publisher.

ISBN: 979-8-89577-611-7 (hardcover)
ISBN: 979-8-89577-699-5 (ebook)

For more information, write to Bearport Publishing, 3500 American Blvd W, Suite 150, Bloomington, MN 55431.
Printed in the United States of America.

CONTENTS

MATH MATTERS!

Have you ever sat in class and wondered . . .

. . . why do I need to learn this?

If you have ever thought that about math, you might be surprised! Math is a big part of your life beyond the classroom.

We use math to count money, tell time, cook food, play games, and much more. Whether or not you know it, math is probably part of some of your favorite things!

LEARNING MATH

Math is all about numbers. We do calculations to figure out how much of things there are. When we write out these calculations, special symbols help us show what we are doing with the numbers.

These blocks show the symbols for adding, subtracting, multiplying, and dividing.

When you learn math, you start by counting. Then, you learn how to do calculations. These skills come in handy when you use math in real life.

What are some ways you use math?

BUILD YOUR SKILLS

Doing math can make you a better problem-solver. It helps you to think **logically**. There are lots of fun ways to strengthen your math skills and watch them grow!

Math is part of lots of games, such as Chutes and Ladders and Monopoly.

Try playing a game that uses numbers or counting. There are lots of math puzzles you could try, too.

EXPERTS AT WORK

Math is an important part of many exciting **careers**.

Astronomers study space. They use math to work out how far away stars and planets are.

Computer **programmers** use math to make websites, apps, and video games.

Meteorologists use a type of math called **statistics** to understand weather.

Architects use math to draw and make buildings.

Engineers use math to solve problems.

Math is part of almost every job you can have.

COUNTING MONEY

Have you ever gone shopping? You probably did math at the store! We add up the prices of the things we buy to find the total cost.

Doing calculations in your head is called mental math.

If you want to buy something special, you may need to save up. Use math to keep track of your money. Subtract the amount of money you have from the cost of what you want to buy. That's how much money you still need.

A calculator can help you solve math problems more easily.

KEEPING TRACK OF TIME

Math is also a part of telling time. Clocks use numbers to show the time of day by the hour and minute. Calendars use numbers to show what day of the month it is.

60 seconds in a minute

60 minutes in an hour

24 hours in a day

7 days in a week

365 days in a year

12 months in a year

How many months and days is it until your next birthday?

COOKING AND BAKING

It even takes math to cook and bake! We use math to make sure we have the right amount of each **ingredient**. We put the ingredients together to make a dish.

Division means splitting a whole into parts. If you want to share a pizza with your friends, you can use division to split it fairly!

This pizza has been divided into six equal slices.

FUN WITH MATH

Math comes in handy in lots of sports and games.

Weight lifters calculate how much weight they can safely add for each lift.

Race car drivers have to understand all of the numbers about their speed, car **temperature**, and lap times.

Pool players use knowledge of **angles** to knock balls in different directions.

Baseball players use math to add up scores and track their statistics.

MEASURING

Measuring means finding out the size, weight, or amount of something. We measure lots of different things. When building, we measure parts to make sure that they will fit together.

We measure things in different units, such as inches or centimeters.

We can measure ourselves, too! You can measure your height to see how much you grow over time. You can measure your foot to find the right shoe size!

How tall are you?

PRACTICING MATH

Math is an important part of our daily lives. We need it to count, measure, buy things, tell time, and much more! Practicing math can be fun.

What are some ways you have used math today?

You can strengthen your math skills by using mental math instead of a calculator. Or you can put your number knowledge to use by learning a new game. There are so many ways to use math beyond the classroom!

Playing a game of darts is a fun way to practice adding.

GLOSSARY

angles the distances between connecting lines

careers jobs that people have for a long time

ingredient one part of a mixture

logically based on reasons that can be proven

programmers people who write instructions for what a computer should do

statistics numbers that show how much or often something happens

temperature how hot or cold something is

INDEX